T0195774

WALKING TOGETHER IN
SOLIDARITY
and
SOLITUDE

CHARLES "HOBS" HOBGOOD

authorHOUSE

AuthorHouse™
1663 Liberty Drive
Bloomington, IN 47403
www.authorhouse.com
Phone: 1 (800) 839-8640

Published by AuthorHouse 07/13/2020

ISBN: 978-1-7283-6670-8 (sc)
ISBN: 978-1-7283-6669-2 (e)

Library of Congress Control Number: 2020912056

Print information available on the last page.

Any people depicted in stock imagery provided by Getty Images are models, and such images are being used for illustrative purposes only. Certain stock imagery © Getty Images.

This book is printed on acid-free paper.

Contents

Author's Notes

There is a space between the implications and inferences of the writer and the interpretations and take away of the reader where mystics are born.

This poetry attempts to be such a garden. Words gathered together in hope that readers will find insights for themselves. A call to move a few steps beyond our cultural conventions and ask new question of ourselves and our world.

The poems are both familiar and fresh and speak to interconnectedness.

They are intended to sustain and deepen our intuitive and spiritual journey.

My hope is that sitting with them you will be called to new challenges.

Charles S Hobgood
chobgood@defiance.edu
Therapist, Educator, Poet
Professor Emeritus Defiance College
Faculty American Youth Foundation-National Leadership Conference
Passion for Spiritual Journey

With Gratitude

Linda Hobgood for spending hours editing these words with love and skill.

She corrected hundreds of punctuation errors but more importantly found words that brightened and illuminated ideas and messages.

John Lacher my friend and technological guide without his input this project would have died on the vine.

Marabeth Hobgood my wife who facilitates even my wildest adventure with support and guard-rails. She is the wind beneath my wings and I cherish her dearly!

Emerson my dog who gives far more than she ever asks.

Dedication

Our daughter Laurie Gregory and husband Mark
Parents of grandchildren: Ryan, Evan, and Lauren

Our son Todd Hobgood and his wife Katie
Parents of grandchildren: Peyton and Madelyn

Lights in our world!

Abstractions Taste Funny

As we stand before the altar of modernization
We must ask, " Are we too late for anything but regret?"
Do we no longer see the fragile web
of interdependence that held the premodern world together
Lives in close knit households and communities
Abandoned for abstractions and the draw of money?
In the old days, learning was an act
of meditation on experience, always an action-
not just an idea or abstraction-
Sure, there is a place for book learning
Especially if you're held up deep
in the stacks of an old library,
Something elementary about being rooted
in ancient earth or old dusty books.

I love my wife by cooking her good food,
She loves me by placing toilet paper on the holder.
Love is more than a Hallmark card or
jewelry ordered on Amazon.
Love like a fresh spring daisy needs to be born
out of germination and then blossom.
Membership use to mean tight, local, close at hand
At the altar of modernization we are struggling to make
face-timing a substitute for a hand held
A voicemail a substitute for a meal dropped off.

Perhaps, perhaps but what am I to do?
When my educated children live in Wisconsin
and Arizona and I live where we hail from in Ohio
Abstractions do not smell like warm peach cobbler
and taste funny, too.

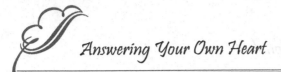

A bright red tail coat
Adorn in gold trim
A black top hat
The ringmaster
A master of hyperbole
Calls your attention to the center ring
Where the world's greatest is holding forth

The consumer master calls your attention
To transform your self-worth
Everything you've ever needed
To be or have he can sell you
To be the center of your own world
An object of envy for others

Only how does the consumer master
Even know what I need
Does he even consider
I may already have what I need?

Is he promising an inner feeling of abundance?
Is he promising enough understanding of the world
that I can feel connected to all living things?
Does he not know that inside my heart
are inexhaustible treasures?
Does he not know that all I need do is place
the consumer master on hold and
answer my heart's call, " I am here".

Astonished

When the Buddha bell stops vibrating where is the sound?
Where do I wake up knowing I have always been there?
Where is that place called deep home?
The place where every corner of the world
has agreed to meet?
The place where everything is one?
To be awake- -to be astonished.

At Seventy

At seventy I am coming to embrace
the art of living into it.
Realizing at times my thoughts
are not much better than
yesterday's lottery ticket.

My motto becomes savor and gaze
Watch the sunset as if it is only the two of you
To experience whole-hog.
To merge with the deer in the meadow
seeing life through his enormous dark eyes
To dance on the razors edge
To listen to life speaking another language
The bearable lightness of being.

Bathsheba

David saw Bathsheba bathing on the roof
and her beauty overcame him
A story of jealousy, deceit, murder and recovery.

Certainly sexuality is a form of beauty
What about sunsets radiating off the mountains
Driving down from Taos to Santa Fe
The moon rising over San Francisco Bay
Milk-colored water tumbling from melting glaciers
A Hawk soaring to catch a Salmon
on the Columbia River
The sound of giant waves crashing on boulders
off the Big Sur Highway.
.

The sun creates great shadows you can walk in
Night brings darkness with an uncontainable mystery
A wide world to live in, to disappear in.
Stretch a little bit more
Am I a spring Robin, a light snow or a song
Circling within the universe
Loving life in an open-hearted way
Impermanent a sweet nectar.

To lose your self in a fabricated world
Being occupied by the mundane
Convention the burial ground
for artful living
There exists a great vortex of false promises.

Follow the difficult trail
Ripen like a seed in fertile ground
Love the question and not the answer
Learn to live into the questions
Watching your self grow takes patience.

Dangerous Questions

Is high energy high because we make it high?
Lipstick and rouge are not just make-up
But tools for brightening the face
We're not just dressed for success
We're dressed in the colors of joy
As if the colors in my scarf will lift your spirits
Every once in a while when I am ready
for a high energy moment
I sneak in the side door of the black church
A spiritual center for high energy making
Now you and I know that privileged folks
have quenched those fires in every way possible
Yet even in the darkest hour
a jazz band leads the afterlife parade
down the back alley to the church
A celebration meal, grits, creole,
shrimp and gravy
Ask yourself, is high energy high
because we make it high?
Ask yourself, is life more about how we respond
than what happens?
These are dangerous questions!

Dictionary Aside

The two greatest
English words
Summer afternoon

Served brimming
in tall glasses
of sweet mint tea

Under umbrellas
Yellow and green
Wind worn

Accompanied by
wordless songs
of rhythmic surf

Laughing Gulls glide
on currents of air
mirroring contentment

Time drifts easy
healing old bones
scarred by harsher days

Worldly concerns
disappear in
sun-bleached sand

Long summer afternoons
fortify us for
life's winters

Gathering Nourishment

Spiritual stewardship honors tradition
While dancing on new horizons
Beyond pathological impatience
The road to contemplation is time.

A hen only lays one egg per day
While feeding all day long
So as to be able to lay tomorrow
Then sits on her nest.

Trail blazers move slowly
Looking for broken twigs
Foot prints in damp moss
Birds' songs echoing off hillsides.

On my walks, in the shower, exhausted in my chair
The spirit of freedom makes space
Asking me to sit, feed, and nest
To give birth only to this moment.

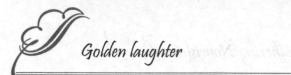

Golden laughter

In the midst of great reoccurring sorrows
Golden laughter
Diminutive laughter
Not disruptive laughter.

The deep laughter of life embracing life
A small gentle gesture strong enough to sustain
Giving birth to hope
Like smiling through tears.

A smile that says, "yes to life"
A smile that says, "I will"
A smile that says,"amen to the cosmos"
A smile that says, " as fleeting as life is it matters" .

Grace and Graveyards

Grace comes
not because someone died for us
But because without it
we would all be dead already
We are marred members of a community
Yet each essential to it
Living for a moment
in a point in time
Part of an underground stream
flowing in all directions

Try walking late at night
through the local graveyard
down by the creek that
runs through the Live Oak grove
Listen, the mute stones are talking.

Growing Edges

Stepping into my own margins
The edge of my comfort zone
Where light shines in dark corners.

Entering a dark pub
Where shaggy bearded men
Sit at round tables
with pints of dark ale
Men who hold very different views.
These men tell their own stories
Stories of abuse, achievement,
failure, heroism and heartbreak
Listening night after night
I can no longer see
them as wrong or even different.
These stories are real, complex, confused
and beautiful.
We are all each other's stories
as much as we are all stardust
Bit players in the drama
In the inexhaustible staging of forever.

Your part is fleeting
Each part an essential moment
in the mystery of time

Harsh Living

We all lean a little off plumb
Swaying to the music
of a manipulating song.
Songs played on
jukeboxes for profit
Songs leading us like sheep
to green pastures to fatten us,
Drunk on the elixirs of illusion
Ready to follow the wrong God home
Sliding from off plumb to crazy.

It's a struggle to keep from being
overwhelmed by the tribe.
Being yourself is harsh living
You will be lonely, frightened,
and tossed around
Yet, no price is too high for the
privilege of finding yourself.

Hero's journey

When a man forgets what is immeasurable
and fails to listen for the song in every silence
only a great homecoming can rescue him from that abyss

40, 000 commercials a week can lead even a monk
to sell his prayer shawl for a fake rainbow.
Beware of talking snakes selling apples on the cheap
Paradise lost an old familiar story
Each of us must and will leave home
in our quest of the holy grail, our faith tested
dragons slain, cities lain barren, mountains climbed,
friends lost and found, all part of the hero's journey.
Yet, even the greatest among us can sleep through the night
until he closes his eyes back where he began
and hears the song in every silence.
.

Holding Ground

Place is where what lies inside of us
communes with what seems outside,
A living frontier where voices come
from place and us as one
A companionship of presence
The raw coming together of us
and the natural world.
Finding our place gives birth
to a living conversation about
what is big and ultimate
Each privileged to be with the other,
A holding ground to drop anchor
Our sanctuary and refuge
when turbulent winds blow.

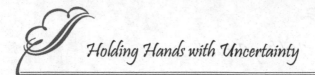

Holding Hands with Uncertainty

As a child I held hands with uncertainty
Delighted in the surprise of not knowing
Giggled when my mom played peek-a-boo
Held my breath twisting the handle
on the Jack-in the-box
Wondered who would dart across in Red Rover
And loved playing Hide and Seek at twilight

Somewhere around ten
Surprise became anxiety
Not knowing turned to fear
Would I get laughed at for my answer?
Are plaid shirts still in?
What would happen if I had animals on my socks?

All of this long before corporate America told me
There are clear winners and losers
Years later sitting on my front porch
A plaid wool blanket draped over my lap
even covering my sagging mismatched socks
Knowing that like October's leaves
I could fall at any time

I delight again in holding hands
with uncertainty
Will someone tell me I had
pizza last night for dinner because
the sauce is all over my shirt

Once again I delight in the surprise
of not knowing
Shame and embarrassment
sleep in a chair in the attic
God is surprise
Peek-a-boo depends upon uncertainty

Safety is an illusion
Only offered to a few

My grandmother at age 11
Witness a lynching

My mother as a young girl
Saw the klan burning crosses.

We are the products
Of those who survive.

Today at the crossroad
Lest we not fall into the worst
of who we are

Call me back
From my anger and chaos.

Let me be brave enough
to knock on the door of other
To find a way to enter other's world
not to join, but to understand.

Time is not money
Time moves at the speed of trust

It is hard to be patient
in what seems a crisis

Land over-plowed will not be
fertile next spring

Standing at the edge
of an over-used field
Ask not, "what can you produce
but what can I do for you"?

Our job is not to export
the task of being human
to experts and institutions

They are what has brought us here.
Each must look to ourselves

Clap your hands and sing
Like the slaves working the fields
Talking in codes, singing of hope.

Just a step or two beyond or behind
what you thought known
No longer clinging to old ways
or even older ideas.
Aging foundations have new cracks
Light shines through broken windows
Shadows no longer daunting
New friends invite laughter
Seeing the silliness of declaring
"If there is is a God?", I'll bet she surprises
both herself and me

Lamentations

Beneath the issue
When schemes and plans
are packed away,
When the idea of this ideology
and that ideology
can no longer be remembered,
When we have lamented long enough
that are sorrow became dust
and in that dust songs begin to grow
Then we may speak of
"the beloved community".

Laurel Mountains

Even after I no longer live here
These Laurel Mountains remain
a cherished companion
These spiritual landscapes
fit in my pocket like a small compass
grounding my life.
We got married at the top of these mountains
in a chapel my grandfather helped build
as did our daughter.
Coming home on holidays became a spiritual pilgrimage
to the "God's Rock" in the green cathedral at Jumonville
Drinking its sustaining water a physical symbol
of the deeper heritage that pulsed through our lives.
A heritage of ever widening circles
Released from the cage unrealized
No longer praying to a narrow God
my spiritual appetite danced with an all-inclusive God
The radical interdependence of life roars like the waters
rushing turbulently downstream.
What gives life its fullness?
A stubborn wild love for living
An immense longing to taste each drop
The river laughs with gladness.

Morning Walks

In stillness of night's
ashen shadows
Just before morning's light
when the sun has yet
to warm the earth

Silhouettes of trees
join earth and sky
each stem faintly visible
A solitary bird cries into dawn
sound echoes down the river

Here a quiet of descending
stairs leads to my inner self
A sacred place of serenity
where God's voice lives in me

Quiet morning walks
Awaken our deepest musings
Whispering loudly
to a sleeping world

Right below the obvious
Something exquisite
Glitters and glows
An ordinary day
Seen through fresh eyes
A butterfly lands on a bright yellow tulip
A praying mantis crawls on the sidewalk
Kindness in your morning coffee
Children skipping

Shadows/light
Yin/yang
Today/yesterday

An old lady at the bar
Grey hair in a bun
Orders a double shot
The man to her left
Stares at her cleavage
Dreams of being younger
Across town a banker
Smiles approving a young couple's mortgage
Sips coffee, foreclosing on a four generation farm
In the corner office at the stadium
The quarterback gets an extension on his 23 million dollar
    contract
At the local hotel the maid cleans her twenty-third room
at minimum wage

The earth spins on its axis
The sun gives light to the moon
Given the gift of life
Short and fleeting
Right below the obvious
Something exquisite
Glitters and glows
An ordinary day

Ordinary day 2

On an ordinary day
Will you come and sit by me?
Down by the Yough River
Share a cup of hot spiced tea
Drop a twig in the river and watch it go
Carried by current to wherever things go
Where our love came from and will return
All the aches and awes of a life together
Will you come and sit by me
Down by the Yough River
Share a cup of hot spiced tea
Side by side breathing in and out

Ordinary day 3

Could there be anything more beautiful
Than an ordinary day?
As night closes dawn comes home
Burnt orange and yellow
Signals the Morning Dove to sing
Silhouettes of trees reflect on the water's edge
as the fog lifts and goes to where fog goes.
I gather myself and walk along the banks
As thousands have done before me
for thousands of years.
I wonder how they spent their holy days
Did they hear the magic haunting sounds
of loons flying overhead?
Did they live their lives as sacraments
or chase wild elusive things ?
I pray they found quiet moments
under star-filled nights
And with each turning of the earth
and dawn's return they saw nothing
can be more beautiful than an ordinary day.

.

At the end of an ordinary day
I built a small fire in the earth's belly
Alongside my camper in Wendy World.
It was late enough that the breeze slept
The day-blind stars came out from hiding
Stillness pulsed in the air.
On these fall nights a small fire
edges out the blossoming chill
Awake my thoughts doze off
A few sparks drift skyward
My gaze follows them into vastness
The fire crackles and my eyes return to the fire.
Losing track of time, the fire becomes embers
Small logs become charred bones blackened and wrinkled
Returning to the earth soil for new growth
I step up on my camper deck open the door to my FB 22
Emerson, my springer spaniel, follows.
We both crawl into our toasty bed
I close my eyes wondering what sweet, weird,
or scary dreams will follow me into night's world.
In my night's dreams, neurons will spark and crackle
Giving birth to morning and another ordinary day.

Painted Ponies

Born with gifts and flaws, we ride.
The merry-go-round of life
goes up and down like painted ponies
The wheels we put in motion
will bring peace or run over us
No matter the effort, life's tragedies
will break our spirit.
Will our hearts
become a thousand broken pieces?
Or will these cracks be
where the light comes in?

Poet's Eyes

Given too much playing time
The conditions given us
can surround and swallow.
To not be eaten alive we need
to enter each day on the edge
of something "crazy or mad"
Something exceptional, excessive,
Outrageous, or unforeseeable
Asking what lies beyond our quest
for profit, winning, or image
Things of immeasurable mystery
Things that linger in obscurity
These are not different things
Rather different ways of looking at things
A poet's eyes see beyond pay-offs,
safety, comfort, or self-interest
When our "poet eyes" close
life becomes flat and tasteless.

Rivers mine the silent stones beneath
simply by doing what rivers do
Doing only their part in the immense cycling of water.
If only we too could learn our part
Simply by doing what we do
we too could mine the stones beneath
finding our depth.

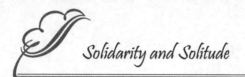

Solidarity and Solitude

Solidarity an act of ripening for the sake of an other
Places a claim on us as if something called us
to a farther horizon.
Holding this difficult claim does not give birth to certainty
Yet we never feel abandon
No longer a heap of half-battered self
Our communion links us
simultaneously beyond and to our selves
Allowing for two solitary individuals
to protect and salute each other

Sweet Confinement

The sweet confinement
of my own aloneness.
Detaching from my littleness
It takes that darkness and risk
to bring the light.

The sweet confinement
of my own aloneness.
Asking myself to subvert the groundings
of everyday conventions and indoctrination.

The sweet confinement
of my own aloneness.
Letting the inner world speak
in its own voice.

The Bend in the Road

The bend in the road
Is a place we
go and where we've
been before and
will go again

A place of sacred
groomed from familiarity
a personal retreat
a healing balm

A place we know
winter, summer,
fall, spring
Watched sun rise,
bleach, and fade

Where feet
meet solid ground
Where muscles taut and tired
unknot, unwind, relax
Where minds cluttered and confused
find solace in solitude

To protect the American way of life
calls for stories that are out of tune
with existing circumstances
Powerful people labeling at their will "fake news"
Like the band playing while the Titanic sank
To not question the way we live
The shadow side of modern life
Economic decline, resource depletion,
Social divide, mass extinction, climate change
A great unraveling.
Before the bow of the Titanic slips from our memory
we all need to post the picture of the earth from the moon
on our computer screen a reminder of
"The Great Turning"

,

A mythic journey
Toward transformation
To rise to the occasion
We must experience rootedness
in something larger than ourselves.
To know the stream of life
running through our veins
Runs through the world
Follow it, the world enriches
If not, the world depletes.

The Point

What is the point because no matter
Bad things happen.
The point- to know the deep truth of who you are
Who you were made to be

Oh you who are nobly born
Having given yourself to love
Which always gives back to you
Know what is wanted for you not from you

No longer burdened by a need
To be worthy
Gifted with the beauty of your own life
Embrace it!!

The Rivers Edge

I too, like the great river, must seek my banks
to find my depth
As Rivers follow their contours
life's journey twists on canvases painted by
choice and nature
Like Rivers flowing toward ever greater sources
life's journey traverses events toward ever greater destinies
an unseen hand acting on our hopes and dreams.

Know the rain falling on a rice field in the pacific rim
will cycle around and moisten a wheat field near Wichita
What could be more exhilarating than being
an essential part of everything and on and on
the journey everlasting

The Size of the House

There is security in knowing
only a corner of the room
A seat by the window
A path to the bathroom.
Not drawing exhaustively from
the magnitude of our own existence
Leaving us strangers to our own lives
Solitude lights our rooms
Solitude is not lonely
It is what we stand on.
These apparently uneventful
moments are the future
happening to us now
Pathways in infinity.
Ancient mystics teach us
what seems alien may become
our best friend
The slain dragon actually the princess.
Resist drawing conclusions hastily
let things simply unfold
A seat by the window
looks out to the world.

Each of us has a thread
Leading to a point beyond words
Where everything of this world
is gone leaving complete emptiness

In a place that seems void
We attach to absolutely everything
Where we begin and end matters not
because God's name is written in us.

Here beyond our will and works
The divine has our personal map.
Hold tight following that thread.
Allow your life to emerge.

You are a seeker
Looking beyond conventional treasures
Guided by the blaze of God's light.
Awake to what is enough.

Treasure Hunt

Finding yourself means being lost.
The only way to reappear is to disappear.
Admit you do not know
and are lousy at predictions.
Life will reveal itself.

To know for even one brief moment
what it means to be free
Never settle for a smaller version of self
Measuring outcomes leads us
away from inner treasures.

# Unspoken

The truth we do not tell
the art of living flies
in the face of success
Retirement the last chance
to move from success to living
To fall in love with Mary Oliver's poems
To long for Wendell Berry's simplicity
To become famous like the button hole to the button
To be moved when the Mountain Laurel blossoms
To hear the butterfly's wing flutter

When will I write a letter
to my deceased grandfather
telling him how his love
for the grain in wood
changed what I valued?
When will I post a picture of my grandchildren
at the soup kitchen on the refrigerator
and not their honor roll article from the newspaper?
When will I stop looking for outcomes
and settle into the impermanent of each moment
and rest in the hands of the Tao?

To live in a frosty world
where folks reside in silos
Isolated by choice
Limits opportunities to see
the difference as richness.
To see the stillness
as the dancing
Solidarity breaks like waves
crashing in a stormy sea
Solitude turns to isolation.
Beauty yet to come, Still
courage comes and goes
Walk together
Life cycles, flower blooms

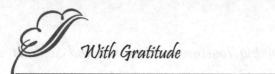

With Gratitude

If the only prayer
I ever utter
Is, "thank you"

It will be
more than enough
even if no earthly person
hears a sound

Gratitude speaks
from the heart

Let the Phone Ring

If you can't climb to the top of the mountain
Then sit, my friend, in a dimly lit pub
A pint of dark ale on the table.
Settle into a well-sculpted question
Engage a patron ready to dig deep.
Open to serendipity
As if both of you have recently returned
from a long adventure, the memory of which has not faded
When was your last really great conversation?
Please, give me a call so we can crawl
into the space between us and bless it
while haunting memories linger.

Liminality

The time and space between
what was and what's next
Waiting, not problem solving
permitting waiting to transform you.
Betwixt and between
Where the old space can fall apart
and a bigger world revealed,
A waiting room where openness and patience
replaces chairs and tables,
No racks of magazines and books.
Just waiting for Dr. Universe
to call us to the changing table
Always a prescription for disruption
Resting in liminality the cloud
of unknowing will lift
and light will break through.

Mountain Paths

Even in the light of day
The woods look dark and deep
Yet walking in
the path opens before us.

The path bends
around a rock ledge
The river appears
class IV and V rapids rumbling.

The path crests the hill
a valley with golden wheat,
clusters of small houses
red barns and cows grazing.

Uncertainty turns with surprise
Life continues to ask
Lace up your shoes
Walk hand-in-hand.

Even in the light of day
The woods look dark and deep
Yet walking in
the path opens before us.

New Church

The name of God
is a fragile flower
crushed under heavy boots
of doctrines, creeds, confessionals
and the institutional church.

For God is the sweet scent
of the flower freely given
and the God in us
our gift freely given.

To be born again is to place
these gifts on the altar of humanity
Resurrection is to be lifted
from centering on our selves.

Ode to a Zip Code

Even before I was born dancing
upside down an embryonic star
My mother meandered around
the kitchen baking brownies and roly-polies
A drawer full of colorful aprons no lady
would wipe her hands on, instead a weekday dress
which later became squares for quilts
on cold winter nights.

Tucked into my second floor bedroom
Looking out over beehive coke ovens
Listening to gears grinding as miners
descended to "Hellish" caverns darker than dark
Little did I know that I was an island child
surrounded by Jews, Catholics, and Coal patch children.

As we clustered at the bus stop closer to my house
forcing Coal Patch Children to long walks
Looking around I saw patch children with
socks for gloves and plastic bags for boots
Schools never closed in 1957 leaving long
waits on snow days with hours to play
Fox and Geese and make snow angels
Time grew friendship and fondness
Fed a sense of social justice.

That same sense of outrage churned my stomach
at the beach in North Carolina when I figured out
what no one had told me that our nanny Josephine

was not allowed in the Atlantic Ocean
That same sense of outrage I experienced this past week
when someone in my adult church class suggested ever so subtly
    that
Injustice is overplayed and there is less violence now than ever
    before.

In those moments I am back at the bus stop
Full of privilege, fur-lined gloves, high top boots,
down filled jacket, and bright colored scarf
Saddened by how little I do
A tear runs slowly down my cheek and
I am not going to justify my behavior
only to say like the Wizard of Oz
"I am not a bad man only a lousy wizard"

None of us knows before we are born
Dancing upside down
Embryonic stars
How much the Zip Code will matter

Open to be Seized

Too many voices inside of me
They give me no rest
I am-I am not
I believe-I believe not
Longing to know, clinging to doubt
What is certain, what is not ?
Where do reason and logic end?
What comes where they stop?

Faced with a spiritual journey
Many different voices calling me home
An inner home of mystery
A home beyond words and space
an altogether different knowing
arrives when reason and logic stop.

Perhaps

We all live in our little village of perhaps
Within the great enormity of cosmic perhaps.
What holds sway is not only the great universe
but the great might be
All of us and everything fueled by hope
All the while hope is calling us
to an unseen future
Whispering in our ear impossible dreams.

Pilgrimage/Anniversary Poem

The smell of incense on our sweaters
Mantras repeating in our ears
A pilgrimage to where the mountains greet the rivers
A journey to find the crack in our being
Where the light comes in.

Calm, clear, open
Stepping stones for this pilgrimage
This adventure an inner journey
An unfolding not a plot or plan
A frequent retreat to Wendy World.

Celtic prayers, Native American flutes,
singing Buddha bowls, chanting the psalms,
silence exploding, whitewater rushing
and a train whistles.

Hot showers, warm blankets, cool night air,
Fresh coffee, fine foods, Irish Cream over French vanilla ice
    cream
long walks, morning fires, and moon beams
shining on the river.

Here at the confluence of the Yough
and the Casselman River
An intersection of two realms
Twilight and dark
Night and dawn
Dreams and sunlight

Sacred transitions offer doorways
To where the light comes in.

Over the hill from our initial vows
Chapel of our ancestors
Down a Mountain Laurel- draped path
to the God's rock
in the midst of a green cathedral.

This place becomes our Jerusalem,
our Mecca, our Santiago
The fertile ground of our aging
Where spiritual sparks
Kindle later life illuminations
Deepening the mystic in each of us
Enriching the confluence of our love.

Pocket Choice

In one pocket I carry a note that says
"I am merely ashes and dust"
In the other pocket I carry a note that says
"The world was made for me"
Somewhere between nothingness and arrogance
I must paddle my canoe
Most days I choose to paddle up stream
Going slow enough to observe my balancing act
Going down stream with the current is exhilarating
Yet dangerous and seductive

Build your hut on the banks
of still waters on sunny days
When your back is strong ride the rapids
The world may not have been made just for you
You were made to be in the world
Tie your life jacket tight

When you think you've left home
You have not gone very far
What is deeply ingrained
just finds another form
Like trees reaching for the sky
Finding expansive views
an inner life that carries you through confusion.
Your journey from a speck of dust
to becoming an elder
Stepping outside narrowness
to living in vastness without explanation

Sitting down by the Yough River
All of this beauty never tries to explain itself
You too try and take in the beauty
for itself without explanation
Minnows darting in shallow water
Fall turning a green world gold.

When you think you've left home
You haven't gone very far
When you've watched the minnows darting
Trying to explain it
Doesn't take you very far
All of this beauty never tries to explain itself
When your tummy growls
It's time to eat.

Winter

Beyond the excitement of the holiday
The early descent of night
Candle on the mantle
Warm smells in the kitchen

Winter wraps generations close
All those before who struggled through the cold
Yet this winter seems extra cold
The embers extra low

At dusk we look toward invisible threads
Foundations of our deeper desires
At times like these we need to unearth
Neglected inner resources

To free ourselves from imprisonment
To find that place where we naturally want to give ourselves
        away
To unlock fingers form the button on the control screen
And wrap them instead around a red ripe tomato

Crush them to make a spicy basil tomato soup
Early nights and warm soup
Sitting in my favorite fireside chair
Gives light to find those invisible threads

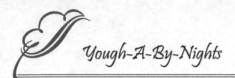
Yough-A-By-Nights

Windows open full
Sounds of whitewater
Fill even the rooms' corners
Ancient rocks and ancient waters
Echoes of a thousand years
Rocked to sleep by timeless music
Healing night sounds
Hearing what is deep and pure
Nature's language in symphony
Grandeur of earth's history
In a single soundscape

Yough Shrine

On my path to the Yough shrine
growing weary I ask my guide
"Where is this shrine"?
He pointed up and down the whole river
and said," the river is the shrine"
The path is not to a destination
the experience is the path and the destination
Along with thousands of side paths
How can a particular shrine be the destination
if everything is sacred ?

Pilgrim pause, fold your hands
Light a candle, look to the hills
You are asked only to walk the path
Signs abound all around
Knowing stays in the mist.

Life a pilgrimage of discovery
Honor the twist and turns
At each bend, at each moment
Find profound companions
fellow travelers among singing birds,
river rocks and crayfish.

Each of us is called
to find the sacred in everyplace and everything
Yet for each of us there is a place called home
A place that both tethers and unleashes us
I call that home the Yough.

Readers Notes

Russian Tales

Printed in the United States
By Bookmasters

Printed in the United States
By Bookmasters